# Friday Nigh Cooking

Delicious and Fast Meals for Friday
Nights
Part 1

By
BookSumo Press

Published by
http://www.booksumo.com

# Table of Contents

Shrimp & Veggies Spring Rolls with Dipping Sauce  5

Chicken, Crab & Veggie Spring Rolls  6

Chicken & Bell Pepper Spring Rolls with Caesar Dressing  7

Shrimp & Vermicelli Spring Rolls with Sauces  8

Classical Pad Thai Noodles I  9

Easy Hummus Thai Style  11

Classical Pad Thai Noodles II  12

Chicken Lo Mein  13

Orange Chicken and Broccoli II  15

Beef and Broccoli I  16

Authentic Fried Rice  17

Authentic Fried Rice II  18

Pepper Steak  19

Egg Foo Yung  20

Chi Tan T'ang  21

Sweet and Spicy Tofu Soup  22

Easy Wonton Soup  23

Alternative Egg Drop Soup  24

Crab Rangoon  25

Chicken Curry I 26

Chicken Curry II 27

Delightfully Thai Basil Chicken 28

Pad Thai III 29

Southeast Asian Chicken Curry 30

Pad Thai III 31

Monterey Shrimp 32

Italian Parmesan Shrimp 33

Louisiana Shrimp 34

Szechwan Shrimp 35

Shrimp Scampi 36

Shrimp Tempura 37

Easy Italian Parmigiana 38

Classical Sausage and Peppers from Italy 39

Easy Biscotti 40

Italian Tuscan Soup 41

Bruschetta 42

Authentic Eggplant Parmesan 43

Classical Risotto 44

Tortellini Classico 45

Feta Fettucine 46

Authentic Meatball Sub  47

Authentic Calamari  48

Northern California Cioppino  49

Classical Fettuccine  50

Plum Tomato and Olive Filets  51

Chicken Cutlets  52

# *Shrimp*
# & Veggies Spring Rolls with Dipping Sauce

Prep Time: 20 mins
Total Time: 50 mins

Servings per Recipe: 6

| | |
|---|---|
| Calories | 59 kcal |
| Fat | 0.3 g |
| Carbohydrates | 8.9 g |
| Protein | 3.4 g |
| Cholesterol | 20 mg |
| Sodium | 168 mg |

## Ingredients

6 spring roll wrappers
12 medium shrimp, cooked and shelled
1 C. shredded leaf lettuce
1/3 C. chopped cilantro
1/2 C. peeled, seeded, chopped cucumber
1 medium carrot, julienned

Quick Thai Dipping Sauce:
1 tbsp light soy sauce
1 tbsp white-wine vinegar or rice vinegar
3 tbsps mirin
1/4 tsp grated ginger root (optional)

## Directions

1. Soak the wrappers, one by one in a bowl of chilled water till limp and transfer onto a smooth surface.
2. In the center of each wrapper, place lettuce, followed by shrimp, cucumber, carrot and cilantro evenly.
3. Roll the wrapper around the filling and with your wet fingers brush the edges and press to seal completely.
4. Place the wrappers onto a large plate and with plastic wrap, cover the rolls and refrigerate before serving.
5. Meanwhile for the dipping sauce in a bowl mix together all the ingredients.
6. Serve the rolls with sauce.

# CHICKEN,
# Crab & Veggie
# Spring Rolls

Prep Time: 20 mins
Total Time: 25 mins

| | |
|---|---|
| Servings per Recipe: 8 | |
| Calories | 208 kcal |
| Fat | 18.8 g |
| Carbohydrates | 7.3g |
| Protein | 4 g |
| Cholesterol | 8 mg |
| Sodium | 71 mg |

## Ingredients

1 quart oil for frying
2 tbsps vegetable oil
1/3 C. shredded cabbage
1/4 C. shredded carrots
1/4 C. shredded cucumber
2 tbsps diced onion
1/4 C. diced green onion
2 tbsps finely chopped shiitake mushrooms
1/3 C. sun-dried tomatoes, chopped

salt and pepper to taste
2 oz. boneless chicken breast halves, cooked and diced
1 oz. cooked crabmeat, diced
1 tsp Chinese five-spice powder
1 avocado - peeled, pitted and diced
1 tsp lemon juice
8 spring roll wrappers

## Directions

1. In a large cast-iron skillet or deep fryer, heat the oil on medium-high heat.
2. In another skillet, heat vegetable oil on medium heat and cook the vegetables with salt and black pepper for about 10 minutes.
3. Add crabmeat, chicken and five-spice powder and stir to combine.
4. Drizzle the avocado with lemon juice and mix it with the chicken mixture.
5. Divide the chicken mixture in the center of each wrapper evenly.
6. Roll the wrapper around the filling and with your wet fingers brush the edges and press to seal completely.
7. Carefully, add the rolls in the skillet in batches.
8. Fry the rolls for about 3 minutes or till golden brown and transfer onto paper towel lined plates to drain.

# *Chicken*
# & Bell Pepper Spring Rolls with Caesar Dressing

Prep Time: 25 mins
Total Time: 25 mins

Servings per Recipe: 4

| | |
|---|---|
| Calories | 230 kcal |
| Fat | 13.8 g |
| Carbohydrates | 15.9 g |
| Protein | 9.6 g |
| Cholesterol | 28 mg |
| Sodium | 327 mg |

## Ingredients

12 rice wrappers (8.5 inch diameter)
1 (5 oz.) package baby romaine lettuce leaves
1 cooked boneless chicken breast half, sliced into thin strips

1 red bell pepper, sliced
1/2 C. Caesar salad dressing

## Directions

1. Soak the wrappers, one by one in a bowl of water till soft and transfer onto a smooth surface.
2. In the center of each wrapper, place some lettuce, followed by chicken strips and bell pepper evenly.
3. Fold the inner sides of the wrappers around the filling and roll tightly.
4. Cut each roll in half and serve with Caesar dressing.

# SHRIMP
# & Vermicelli Spring Rolls with Sauces

<table>
<tr><td>🥣 Prep Time: 45 mins</td></tr>
<tr><td>🕐 Total Time: 50 mins</td></tr>
</table>

| Servings per Recipe: 8 | |
|---|---|
| Calories | 82 kcal |
| Fat | 0.7 g |
| Carbohydrates | 15.8g |
| Protein | 3.3 g |
| Cholesterol | 11 mg |
| Sodium | 305 mg |

## Ingredients

For Rolls:
2-oz. rice vermicelli
8 (8 1/2-inch) rice wrappers
8 large cooked shrimp, peeled, deveined and halved
3 tbsps fresh cilantro, chopped
3 tbsps fresh mint leaves
1 1/3 tbsps fresh Thai basil leaves, chopped
2 lettuce leaves, chopped
For Sauces:

1 tsp peanuts, chopped finely
3 tbsps hoisin sauce
1/4 C. water
2 tbsps white sugar
1 garlic clove, minced
2 tbsps fresh lime juice
1/2 tsp garlic chili sauce

## Directions

1. In a pan of boiling water, add the vermicelli and cook for about 3-5 minutes or till desired doneness. Drain well.
2. Soak the wrappers, one by one in a bowl of warm water for 1 second or till soft and transfer onto a smooth surface.
3. In the center of each wrapper, place the shrimp, followed by the vermicelli, fresh herbs and lettuce evenly.
4. Fold the inner sides of the wrappers around the filling and roll tightly.
5. Meanwhile for first sauce in a bowl mix together the peanuts and hoisin sauce.
6. In another bowl mix together the remaining ingredients.
7. Serve these rolls with both sauces.

# Classical
# Pad Thai Noodles I

🥣 Prep Time: 30 mins
🕐 Total Time: 2 hrs

| Servings per Recipe: 4 | |
|---|---|
| Calories | 397 kcal |
| Carbohydrates | 39.5 g |
| Cholesterol | 41 mg |
| Fat | 23.3 g |
| Protein | 13.2 g |
| Sodium | 1234 mg |

## Ingredients

2/3 cup dried rice vermicelli
1/4 cup peanut oil
2/3 cup thinly sliced firm tofu
1 large egg, beaten
4 cloves garlic, finely chopped
1/4 cup vegetable broth
2 tbsps fresh lime juice
2 tbsps soy sauce
1 tbsp white sugar
1 tsp salt

1/2 tsp dried red chili flakes
3 tbsps chopped peanuts
1 pound bean sprouts, divided
3 green onions, whites cut thinly across and greens sliced into thin lengths - divided
3 tbsps chopped peanuts
2 limes, cut into wedges for garnish

## Directions

1.  Put rice vermicelli noodles in hot water for about 30 minutes before draining the water.
2.  Cook tofu in hot oil until golden brown before draining it with paper tower.
3.  Reserve 1 tbsp of oil for later use and cook egg in the remaining hot oil until done, and set them aside for later use.
4.  Now cook noodles and garlic in the hot reserved oil, while coating them well with this oil along the way.
5.  In this pan containing noodles; add tofu, salt, chili flakes, egg and 3 tbsps peanuts, and mix all this very thoroughly.
6.  Also add bean sprouts and green onion into it, while reserving some for the garnishing purposes.
7.  Cook all this for two minutes before transferring to a serving platter.

8. Garnish this with peanuts and the reserved vegetables before placing some lime wedges around the platter to make this dish more attractive.

9. Serve.

# *Easy*
# Hummus Thai Style

🥣 Prep Time: 15 mins
🕐 Total Time: 30 mins

Servings per Recipe: 12
| | |
|---|---|
| Calories | 142 kcal |
| Carbohydrates | 13.8 g |
| Cholesterol | 0 mg |
| Fat | 9.4 g |
| Protein | 3.9 g |
| Sodium | 315 mg |

## Ingredients

1/4 cup coconut oil
2 large cloves garlic, very thinly sliced
2 cups cooked garbanzo beans
1/4 cup fresh lime juice
1/4 cup peanut butter
1/4 cup coconut milk
1/4 cup sweet chili sauce
1/4 cup minced lemon grass

1/4 cup minced fresh Thai basil leaves
1 tbsp grated fresh ginger
2 tsps green curry paste
1 jalapeno pepper, minced
1/2 tsp salt
1 pinch cayenne pepper(optional)
1 pinch chili powder (optional)

## Directions

1. Cook garlic in hot coconut oil for about one minute and transfer it to a bowl.
2. Put cooled garlic mixture, lime juice, coconut milk, chili sauce, lemon grass, basil, ginger, curry paste, garbanzo beans, jalapeno pepper, salt, peanut butter, cayenne pepper and chili in a blender and blend it until you find that it is smooth. Serve.

# CLASSICAL
# Pad Thai Noodles II

🥣 Prep Time: 15 mins
🕐 Total Time: 25 mins

Servings per Recipe: 4
Calories            352 kcal
Carbohydrates       46.8 g
Cholesterol         46 mg
Fat                 15 g
Protein             9.2 g
Sodium              335 mg

## Ingredients

1 (6.75 ounce) package thin rice noodles
2 tbsps vegetable oil
3 ounces fried tofu, sliced into thin strips
1 clove garlic, minced
1 egg
1 tbsp soy sauce
1 pinch white sugar
2 tbsps chopped peanuts
1 cup fresh bean sprouts

1 tbsp chopped fresh cilantro
1 lime, cut into wedges

## Directions

1. In a heatproof bowl containing noodles, pour boiling water and let it stand as it is for about five minutes before draining the water and setting it aside for later use.
2. Fry garlic in hot oil until brown before adding noodles frying it for about one minute.
3. Now add egg into it and break it up when it starts to get solid, and mix it well into the noodles.
4. Now add soy sauce, tofu, cilantro, bean sprouts, sugar and peanuts into it and mix it well.
5. Remove from heat and add lime wedges just before you serve

# Chicken
# Lo Mein

Prep Time: 40 mins
Total Time: 2 hrs 15 mins

Servings per Recipe: 4
| | |
|---|---|
| Calories | 603 kcal |
| Fat | 14.9 g |
| Carbohydrates | 78.9g |
| Protein | 38.3 g |
| Cholesterol | 62 mg |
| Sodium | 2177 mg |

## Ingredients

4 skinless, boneless chicken breast halves - cut into thin strips
5 tsps white sugar, divided
3 tbsps rice wine vinegar
1/2 C. soy sauce, divided
1 1/4 C. chicken broth
1 C. water
1 tbsp sesame oil
1/2 tsp ground black pepper
2 tbsps cornstarch

1 (12 oz.) package uncooked linguine pasta
2 tbsps vegetable oil, divided
2 tbsps minced fresh ginger root
1 tbsp minced garlic
1/2 lb fresh shiitake mushrooms, stemmed and sliced
6 green onions, sliced diagonally into 1/2 inch pieces

## Directions

1. Get a bowl, mix: 1/4 C. soy sauce, chicken, 1.5 tbsps vinegar, and 2.5 tsps sugar.
2. Place a covering of plastic around the bowl and put everything in the fridge for 60 mins.
3. Get a 2nd bowl, mix: black pepper, broth, sesame oil, and water.
4. Now combine both bowls.
5. Get a 3rd bowl and mix a small amount of the contents from the 2nd bowl with your cornstarch until everything is smooth.
6. Then combine everything together into 1 bowl.
7. Boil your pasta in water and salt for 9 mins, then remove all the liquids.
8. At the same time begin to stir fry your chicken in 1 tbsp of veggie oil for 6 mins and then place it to

the side.

9.  Add in the rest of the oil and fry the following for 2 mins: green onions, ginger mushrooms, and garlic.

10. Combine in the cornstarch mix and the chicken and cook everything for 3 mins until it all becomes thick.

11. Now add the pasta and toss the contents.

12. Enjoy.

# Orange Chicken and Broccoli II

Prep Time: 20 mins
Total Time: 40 mins

Servings per Recipe: 4
Calories         380 kcal
Fat              14 g
Carbohydrates    33.1g
Protein          31.7 g
Cholesterol      68 mg
Sodium           938 mg

## Ingredients

1/2 C. orange juice
3 tbsps soy sauce
3 cloves garlic, diced
1 tbsp grated orange zest
1 tsp ground ginger
1/2 tsp red pepper flakes (optional)
3 tbsps vegetable oil
4 skinless, boneless chicken breast halves, thinly sliced
1/2 C. chicken broth
2 tbsps cornstarch

1 (16 oz.) package frozen stir-fry vegetables
1 C. sugar snap peas
1 C. broccoli florets
1 C. sliced carrot

## Directions

1. Get a bowl, combine: pepper flakes, orange juice, ginger, soy sauce, orange zest, and garlic.
2. Get your oil hot and then begin to stir fry your chicken and orange mix for 12 mins.
3. Get a 2nd bowl, combine: the cornstarch and broth.
4. Add this mix to the chicken, gradually, to make the sauce thicker.
5. Once the mix has reached a consistency that you prefer add: carrots, veggies, broccoli, and snap peas.
6. Continue frying and stirring the contents for 9 more mins.
7. Enjoy.

# BEEF
# and Broccoli I

Prep Time: 10 mins
Total Time: 1 hr 10 mins

Servings per Recipe: 4
Calories            665 kcal
Carbohydrates       104.6 g
Cholesterol         39 mg
Fat                 13.8 g
Protein             30.5 g
Sodium              1594 mg

## Ingredients

2 cups brown rice
4 cups water
2 tbsps cornstarch
2 tsps white sugar
6 tbsps soy sauce
1/4 cup white wine
1 tbsp minced fresh ginger
1 pound boneless beef round steak, cut into thin strips
1 tbsp vegetable oil
3 cups broccoli florets

2 carrots, thinly sliced
1 (6 ounce) package frozen pea pods, thawed
2 tbsps chopped onion
1 (8 ounce) can sliced water chestnuts, undrained
1 cup Chinese cabbage
2 large heads bok choy, chopped
1 tbsp vegetable oil

## Directions

1. Get your rice boiling in water, set the heat to low, cover the pan, and let the rice cook for 40 mins until done.
2. Get a bowl, combine the following ingredients: soy sauce, cornstarch, wine, and sugar.
3. Mix everything evenly then add the ginger and beef to the marinade.
4. Get a wok and heat 1 tsp oil. Begin to stir fry for 1 min: onions, broccoli, pea pods, and carrots.
5. Mix in: bok choy, Chinese cabbage, and the water chestnuts.
6. Place a lid on the pan and let everything fry for 4 mins.
7. Now remove everything from the pan and add in 1 tsp oil.
8. Begin to fry the beef for 4 mins. Then add the veggies back into the mix and continue frying everything for 3 more mins. Enjoy with cooked brown rice.

# Authentic
# Fried Rice

Prep Time: 25 mins
Total Time: 1 hr 20 mins

Servings per Recipe: 6
| | |
|---|---|
| Calories | 415 kcal |
| Carbohydrates | 12.6 g |
| Cholesterol | 64.8g |
| Fat | 12.9 g |
| Protein | 562 mg |
| Sodium | 415 kcal |

## Ingredients

2 C. uncooked white rice
4 C. water
4 dried shiitake mushrooms, cleaned
1 C. hot water
1/2 lb ground chicken
1 tbsp soy sauce
1 tsp sesame oil
1 pinch white pepper
2 tbsps vegetable oil

3 cloves garlic, sliced
2 links lop chong (Chinese-style sausage), thinly sliced
1 tbsp dark soy sauce
4 green onions, diced
2 eggs, lightly beaten

## Directions

1. Get your rice boiling in 4 C. of water.
2. Once the mix is boiling set the heat to low, place a lid on the pot, and let the rice cook for 22 mins.
3. Now begin to soak your mushrooms in hot water for 12 mins. Then dice the mushrooms and keep the liquid.
4. Get a bowl, combine: chicken, white pepper, sesame oil, and soy sauce
5. Begin to stir fry your garlic in veggie oil for 4 mins then add: sausage, mushrooms, and chicken.
6. Stir the mix until the chicken is fully done then add in: the rice, mushroom liquid, green onions, and soy sauce.
7. Continue stir frying until everything is coated with sauce.
8. Then add the eggs on top of everything and keep stir frying until the eggs are firm.
9. Enjoy.

# AUTHENTIC
# Fried Rice II

🥄 Prep Time: 5 mins
🕐 Total Time: 15 mins

Servings per Recipe: 4

| | |
|---|---|
| Calories | 255 kcal |
| Fat | 10.2 g |
| Carbohydrates | 25.9 g |
| Protein | 14.1 g |
| Cholesterol | 83 mg |
| Sodium | 516 mg |

## Ingredients

1 egg
1 tbsp water
1 tbsp butter
1 tbsp vegetable oil
1 onion, diced
2 C. cooked white rice, cold
2 tbsps soy sauce

1 tsp ground black pepper
1 C. cooked, diced chicken meat

## Directions

1. Get a bowl, combine: water and whisked eggs.
2. Get some butter hot in a frying pan then pour in your eggs.
3. Let the eggs sit for 3 mins then remove the eggs and cut them into strips.
4. Now being to stir fry your onions, until they are soft, in the same pan, then add in the chicken, rice, pepper, and soy sauce.
5. Cook the mix, while stirring, for 7 mins then add in the eggs and continue cooking everything for 2 more mins.
6. Enjoy.

# *Pepper* Steak

🥣 Prep Time: 15 mins
🕐 Total Time: 30 mins

Servings per Recipe: 4
| | |
|---|---|
| Calories | 312 kcal |
| Fat | 15.4 g |
| Carbohydrates | 17g |
| Protein | 26.1 g |
| Cholesterol | 69 mg |
| Sodium | 972 mg |

## Ingredients

1 lb beef top sirloin steak
1/4 C. soy sauce
2 tbsps white sugar
2 tbsps cornstarch
1/2 tsp ground ginger
3 tbsps vegetable oil, divided
1 red onion, cut into 1-inch squares

1 green bell pepper, cut into 1-inch squares
2 tomatoes, cut into wedges

## Directions

1. Cut your steak into strips.
2. Get a bowl, combine: ginger, soy sauce, cornstarch, and sugar.
3. Combine the mix until the sugar dissolves. Then add in your steak and coat the pieces.
4. Now get 1 tbsp of veggie oil hot in a wok and add in one third of the steak to the pot.
5. Stir fry everything for 5 mins then place the steak into a bowl.
6. Continue frying your steak in thirds and placing the meat in the same bowl
7. Once the steak is cooked add everything back into the pot and also add in your onions.
8. Stir fry the mix for 4 mins then add the green pepper.
9. Continue cooking everything for 3 more mins then add in the tomatoes and get them hot.
10. Enjoy.

# EGG
# Foo Yung

🥘 Prep Time: 10 mins
🕐 Total Time: 30 mins

Servings per Recipe: 2
Calories           328 kcal
Fat                23.8 g
Carbohydrates      13g
Protein            18.1 g
Cholesterol        372 mg
Sodium             11502 mg

## Ingredients

1 large green onion
4 eggs, beaten
3/4 C. bean sprouts
3 tbsps soy sauce, divided
2 tbsps peanut oil, divided

2 C. sliced fresh mushrooms
4 tsps cornstarch
1 C. chicken or beef broth

## Directions

1. Dice your green onions and place 1 tbsp to the side.
2. Now combine the rest of the onions with 1 tbsp soy sauce, bean sprouts, and eggs.
3. Get 1 tbsp of peanut oil hot and add 1/4 a C. of egg mix to the oil.
4. Cook the mix for 3 mins then flip everything and continue cooking the mic for 1 more mins.
5. Place the egg on a plate. And continue cooking the remaining ingredients.
6. Add in 1 more tbsp of peanut oil and stir fry your mushrooms in it with 2 more tbsps of soy sauce for 4 mins.
7. Mix the broth with the cornstarch and add the mix to the mushrooms and let the contents cook until the mix becomes thick.
8. Coat your eggs with the sauce and serve.
9. Enjoy.

# Chi Tan T'ang (Classical Egg Drop Soup)

Prep Time: 10 mins
Total Time: 20 mins

Servings per Recipe: 6
Calories          62 kcal
Fat               2.8 g
Carbohydrates     4.7g
Protein           4.5 g
Cholesterol       94 mg
Sodium            1872 mg

## Ingredients

8 cubes chicken bouillon
6 C. hot water
2 tbsps cornstarch
2 tbsps soy sauce
3 tbsps distilled white vinegar

1 green onion, minced
3 eggs, beaten

## Directions

1. Get a large pot and begin to heat some hot water and bouillon.
2. Stir and heat the mix until the bouillon is completely dissolved.
3. Now add in: the green onions, soy sauce, and vinegar.
4. Get the mix boiling then set the heat to low.
5. Slowly add in your whisked eggs while stirring.
6. Once the eggs have set, shut the heat.
7. Enjoy.

# SWEET AND SPICY
# Tofu Soup

Prep Time: 20 mins
Total Time: 50 mins

Servings per Recipe: 4
| | |
|---|---|
| Calories | 211 kcal |
| Fat | 12 g |
| Carbohydrates | 17.3g |
| Protein | 11.3 g |
| Cholesterol | 0 mg |
| Sodium | 243 mg |

## Ingredients

1 tbsp vegetable oil
1 red bell pepper, diced
3 green onions, diced
2 C. water
2 C. chicken broth
1 tbsp soy sauce
1 tbsp red wine vinegar
1/4 tsp crushed red pepper flakes
1/8 tsp ground black pepper
1 tbsp cornstarch

3 tbsps water
1 tbsp sesame oil
6 oz. frozen snow peas
1 (8 oz.) package firm tofu, cubed
1 (8 oz.) can sliced water chestnuts, drained

## Directions

1. Stir fry your green onions and bell peppers in oil for 7 mins then combine in: soy sauce, broth, and 2 C. of water.
2. Now set the heat to medium and let the mix cook for 7 more mins.
3. Get a bowl, combine: sesame oil, vinegar, 3 tbsps water, pepper flakes, cornstarch, and black pepper.
4. Stir the mix until it is smooth then pour it into the simmering broth.
5. Continue simmering the broth for 7 more mins until it gets thick then add in: water chestnuts, snow peas, and tofu.
6. Let the tofu cook for 12 mins.
7. Enjoy.

# *Easy*
# Wonton Soup

Prep Time: 5 mins
Total Time: 15 mins

Servings per Recipe: 4
Calories            293 kcal
Fat                 9 g
Carbohydrates       33.5g
Protein             17.7 g
Cholesterol         84 mg
Sodium              3373 mg

## Ingredients

8 C. chicken broth
3 tbsps soy sauce
2 tsps sesame oil
2 tsps rice wine vinegar
2 tsps lemon juice
2 tsps minced garlic
1 1/2 tsps chile-garlic sauce (such as Sriracha(R))

salt to taste
8 C. water
20 wontons

## Directions

1. Get the following simmering: salt, broth, chili garlic sauce, sesame oil, garlic, wine vinegar, and lemon juice.
2. Let the mix gently simmer for 12 mins.
3. At the same time being to get some water boiling in another pot. Add the wontons to the boiling water and let the mix cook for 7 mins. Then combine the wontons to the simmering mix.
4. Enjoy.

# ALTERNATIVE
# Egg Drop Soup

Prep Time: 10 mins
Total Time: 20 mins

Servings per Recipe: 4

| | |
|---|---|
| Calories | 36 kcal |
| Fat | 1.6 g |
| Carbohydrates | 4g |
| Protein | 1.7 g |
| Cholesterol | 46 mg |
| Sodium | 164 mg |

## Ingredients

1 egg
1/4 tsp salt
2 tbsps tapioca flour
1/4 C. cold water
4 C. chicken broth
1/8 tsp ground ginger
1/8 tsp minced fresh garlic

2 tbsps diced green onion
1/4 tsp Asian (toasted) sesame oil (optional)
1 pinch white pepper (optional)

## Directions

1. Get a bowl and whisk your eggs with salt in it.
2. Get a 2nd bowl, mix: cold water and tapioca flour. Mix everything until its smooth.
3. Now get your garlic, ginger, and broth boiling.
4. Once the mix has boiled for about 2 mins add the tapioca mix and continue boiling everything for about 2 more mins until the mix is no longer cloudy and thick.
5. Remove the mix from the heat and add the eggs in gradually.
6. Combine the eggs in slowly in the form of a circle but do not stir the mix too much.
7. Once the eggs have set add a garnishing of white pepper, sesame oil, and onions.
8. Enjoy.

# Crab
# Rangoon (Cream Cheese Wontons)

🥣 Prep Time: 15 mins

🕐 Total Time: 25 mins

Servings per Recipe: 10

| | |
|---|---|
| Calories | 312 kcal |
| Fat | 19 g |
| Carbohydrates | 25.6g |
| Protein | 10.4 g |
| Cholesterol | 43 mg |
| Sodium | 491 mg |

## Ingredients

1 quart oil for frying
1 tbsp vegetable oil
1 clove garlic, minced
2 tbsps minced onion
1 medium head bok choy, diced
2 tbsps diced snow peas
1 (6 oz.) can crab meat, drained

1 (8 oz.) package cream cheese, softened
1 tbsp soy sauce
1 (14 oz.) package small won ton wrappers

## Directions

1. Get a large pot or Dutch oven and get your oil hot to 375 degrees before doing anything else.

2. Now being to stir fry your onions and garlic for 3 mins then combine in the pea pods and bok choy.

3. Fry the veggies until they are crisp for a few mins.

4. Now get a bowl, mix: stir fry veggies, crab, soy sauce, and cream cheese.

5. Place a tsp of mix into the middle of your wonton wrapper and from the wrapper into a triangle. Use a bit of water and some pinching to seal the edges.

6. Fry your ragoon in the oil until browned.

7. Enjoy.

# CHICKEN
# Curry I

Prep Time: 15 mins
Total Time: 55 mins

Servings per Recipe: 6
| | |
|---|---|
| Calories | 500 kcal |
| Carbohydrates | 22.1 g |
| Cholesterol | 58 mg |
| Fat | 36.1 g |
| Protein | 25.8 g |
| Sodium | 437 mg |

## Ingredients

3 tbsps Thai yellow curry paste (such as Mae Ploy®)
1 pound cooked skinless, boneless chicken breast, cut into bite-size pieces
2 (14 ounce) cans coconut milk
1 cup chicken stock
1 yellow onion, chopped
3 small red potatoes, cut into cubes, or as needed

3 red Thai chili peppers, chopped with seeds, or more to taste
1 tsp fish sauce

## Directions

1. Mix curry paste in hot oil before adding chicken and coating it well.
2. Add 1 can coconut milk and cook it for five minutes before adding the rest of the coconut milk, onion, potatoes, chicken stock and chili peppers into it and bringing all this to boil.
3. Turn the heat down to low and cook for 25 minutes or until the potatoes are tender.
4. Add fish sauce into before serving.
5. Enjoy.

# Chicken
# Curry II

🥣 Prep Time: 15 mins
🕐 Total Time: 35 mins

Servings per Recipe: 4

| | |
|---|---|
| Calories | 621 kcal |
| Carbohydrates | 86.7 g |
| Cholesterol | 91 mg |
| Fat | 19.4 g |
| Protein | 35.2 g |
| Sodium | 316 mg |

## Ingredients

1 tbsp canola oil
2 tbsps green curry paste
1 pound boneless skinless chicken breasts, cut into bite-size pieces
1 small onion, thinly sliced
1 red pepper, cut into thin strips, then cut crosswise in half

1 green pepper, cut into thin strips, then cut crosswise in half
4 ounces cream cheese, cubed
1/4 cup milk
1/8 tsp white pepper
2 cups hot cooked long-grain white rice

## Directions

1. Combine curry paste and hot oil before adding chicken and onions.
2. Cook this for about 8 minutes before adding green and red peppers, and cooking for another five minutes.
3. Now add cream cheese, white pepper and milk, and cook until you see that the cheese has melted.
4. Serve this on top of rice.
5. Enjoy.

# DELIGHTFULLY
# Delightfully Thai Basil Chicken

Prep Time: 15 mins
Total Time: 20 mins

| Servings per Recipe: 4 | |
| --- | --- |
| Calories | 273 kcal |
| Carbohydrates | 16.5 g |
| Cholesterol | 69 mg |
| Fat | 10.7 g |
| Protein | 29.4 g |
| Sodium | 769 mg |

## Ingredients

2 tbsps peanut oil
1/4 cup minced garlic
1 pound ground chicken breast
12 Thai chilis, sliced into thin rings
2 tsps black soy sauce

2 tbsps fish sauce
1 cup fresh basil leaves

## Directions

1. Cook garlic in hot peanut oil for about twenty seconds before adding ground chicken and cooking for another two minutes or until the chicken loses any pinkness.
2. Now add sliced chilies, fish sauce and soy sauce into it before cooking for 15 seconds to get the chilies tender.
3. At the very end, add basil and cook until you see that basil has wilted.
4. Serve.

# Pad Thai

III

🥣 Prep Time: 30 mins
🕐 Total Time: 30 mins

Servings per Recipe: 4
| | |
|---|---|
| Calories | 452 kcal |
| Fat | 28.6 g |
| Carbohydrates | 45.8g |
| Protein | 13.7 g |
| Cholesterol | 0 mg |
| Sodium | 478 mg |

## Ingredients

2 zucchini, ends trimmed
2 carrots
1 head red cabbage, thinly sliced
1 red bell pepper, thinly sliced
1/2 C. bean sprouts
3/4 C. raw almond butter
2 oranges, juiced

2 tbsps raw honey
1 tbsp minced fresh ginger root
1 tbsp Nama Shoyu (raw soy sauce)
1 tbsp unpasteurized miso
1 clove garlic, minced
1/4 tsp cayenne pepper

## Directions

1. Grab a veggie peeler and cut your zucchini lengthwise.
2. Continue cutting the veggies into long streaks to create ribbons.
3. Create the same type of ribbons with your carrots.
4. Now get a bowl, combine: bean sprouts, carrots, bell peppers, and cabbage.
5. Stir the mix to evenly combine everything.
6. Get a 2nd bowl, combine: cayenne, almond butter, orange juice, garlic, miso, honey, Nama Shoyu, and ginger.
7. Add half of the 2nd bowl to the first bowl and stir the mix to evenly coat the veggies.
8. Add your zucchini to the bowl with the cabbage then top the zucchini with the rest of the sauce.
9. Stir everything to evenly distribute the zucchini throughout.
10. Enjoy.

# SOUTHEAST
# Asian Chicken Curry

🥣 Prep Time: 20 mins
🕐 Total Time: 55 mins

Servings per Recipe: 4
Calories            690 kcal
Fat                 41.2 g
Carbohydrates       47.3g
Protein             38.1 g
Cholesterol         73 mg
Sodium              1221 mg

## Ingredients

2 tbsps vegetable oil
3 tbsps curry paste
1 (3/4 inch thick) slice ginger, minced
1 1/4 lbs skinless, boneless chicken breast meat - cubed
3 tbsps brown sugar
3 tbsps fish sauce

3 tbsps tamarind paste
1/3 C. peanut butter
3 C. peeled, cubed potatoes
1 (13.5 oz.) can coconut milk
3 tbsps fresh lime juice

## Directions

1. Begin to stir fry your ginger and curry paste in veggie oil for 3 mins then add in the chicken and fry everything for 5 mins.

2. Now combine in: the coconut milk, brown sugar, potatoes, fish sauce, peanut butter, and tamarind.

3. Get everything boiling, place a lid on the pot, set the heat to low, and let the mix cook for 22 mins, until the chicken is fully done and the potatoes are soft.

4. Now stir in your lime juice and let the contents cook for 6 more mins.

5. Enjoy.

# Provolone
# Shrimp

🥣 Prep Time: 5 mins
🕐 Total Time: 15 mins

Servings per Recipe: 4
| | |
|---|---|
| Calories | 647 kcal |
| Carbohydrates | 40.4 g |
| Cholesterol | 252 mg |
| Fat | 32.5 g |
| Protein | 47.5 g |
| Sodium | 2513 mg |

## Ingredients

1/4 cup butter
1 tbsp chopped green onion
1 pound fresh shrimp, peeled and deveined
2 tbsps all-purpose flour
2 tbsps Old Bay Seasoning TM
2 cups milk
1 tbsp celery, chopped

1 large tomato, sliced
8 slices provolone cheese
4 English muffins, split and toasted

## Directions

1. Cook shrimp and onion in hot butter until you see that shrimp are pink before stirring in flour and some old bay seasoning.
2. Now add milk very slowly into the pan, while stirring continuously before adding celery and cooking it until you see that it is soft.
3. Preheat your oven after selecting broiler from the options.
4. Put mixture with the help of spoon into the muffin cups before topping each one with tomato and provolone cheese.
5. Put it under the broiler for about one minute or until you see that cheese has melted.
6. Serve.

# MONTEREY
# Shrimp

🍳 Prep Time: 20 mins

🕐 Total Time: 30 mins

Servings per Recipe: 8
| | |
|---|---|
| Calories | 284 kcal |
| Carbohydrates | 0.4 g |
| Cholesterol | 205 mg |
| Fat | 16.9 g |
| Protein | 30.7 g |
| Sodium | 753 mg |

## Ingredients

1 (8 ounce) package Monterey Jack cheese, cut into strips
40 large shrimp - peeled, deveined and butterflied

20 slices turkey bacon, cut in half

## Directions

1. Set your oven at 450 degrees F.
2. Put cheese along with a slice of bacon in the butter flied opening of each shrimp before placing it on a cookie sheet.
3. Bake this in the preheated oven for about 15 minutes.
4. Serve.

# *Italian*
# Parmesan Shrimp

Prep Time: 10 mins
Total Time: 20 mins

Servings per Recipe: 4
| | |
|---|---|
| Calories | 215 kcal |
| Carbohydrates | 1.9 g |
| Cholesterol | 188 mg |
| Fat | 11.3 g |
| Protein | 26.4 g |
| Sodium | 412 mg |

## Ingredients

2 tbsps olive oil
2 cloves garlic, chopped
1/4 cup chopped green onion
1 pound fresh shrimp, peeled and deveined

1/2 cup Italian flat leaf parsley, chopped
1/2 cup freshly grated Parmesan cheese

## Directions

1. Cook garlic and scallions in hot olive for a minute before adding shrimp and cooking it until pink.
2. Add some parsley and cook until heated through before turning the heat off and adding some grated parmesan cheese.
3. Serve.

# LOUISIANA
# Shrimp

Prep Time: 5 mins
Total Time: 15 mins

Servings per Recipe: 4
| | |
|---|---|
| Calories | 166 kcal |
| Carbohydrates | 0.9 g |
| Cholesterol | 259 mg |
| Fat | 5 g |
| Protein | 28 g |
| Sodium | 443 mg |

## Ingredients

1 tsp paprika
3/4 tsp dried thyme
3/4 tsp dried oregano
1/4 tsp garlic powder
1/4 tsp salt
1/4 tsp ground black pepper
1/4 tsp cayenne pepper, or more to taste

1 1/2 pounds large shrimp, peeled and deveined
1 tbsp vegetable oil

## Directions

1. Coat shrimp with the mixture of paprika, garlic powder, thyme, oregano, salt, pepper, and cayenne pepper in a sealable plastic bag.
2. Now cook this shrimp in the hot oil in a skillet for about four minutes or until you see that it is no longer transparent from the center.
3. Serve.

# Szechwan
# Shrimp

🥣 Prep Time: 10 mins
🕐 Total Time: 20 mins

Servings per Recipe: 4
Calories            142 kcal
Carbohydrates       6.7 g
Cholesterol         164 mg
Fat                 4.4 g
Protein             18.3 g
Sodium              500 mg

## Ingredients

4 tbsps water
2 tbsps ketchup
1 tbsp soy sauce
2 tsps cornstarch
1 tsp honey
1/2 tsp crushed red pepper
1/4 tsp ground ginger

1 tbsp vegetable oil
1/4 cup sliced green onions
4 cloves garlic, minced
12 ounces cooked shrimp, tails removed

## Directions

1. Combine water, crushed red pepper, ketchup, soy sauce, cornstarch, honey and ground ginger in a medium sized bowl and set it aside.
2. Cook green onions and garlic in hot oil for about 30 seconds before adding shrimp and mixing it well.
3. Now add sauce and cook until you see that the sauce has thickened.
4. Serve.

# SHRIMP
# Scampi

Prep Time: 15 mins
Total Time: 25 mins

Servings per Recipe: 4
| | |
|---|---|
| Calories | 606 kcal |
| Carbohydrates | 35.5 g |
| Cholesterol | 247 mg |
| Fat | 30.8 g |
| Protein | 35.3 g |
| Sodium | 680 mg |

## Ingredients

1 (8 ounce) package angel hair pasta
1/2 cup butter
4 cloves minced garlic
1 pound shrimp, peeled and deveined
1 cup dry white wine

1/4 tsp ground black pepper
3/4 cup grated Parmesan cheese
1 tbsp chopped fresh parsley

## Directions

1. Cook pasta in boiling salty water until tender before draining it.
2. Now cook shrimp and garlic in hot butter over medium for about three minutes before adding wine and pepper, and cooking all this for another 30 seconds.
3. Now combine pasta and shrimp in a bowl before adding cheese and parsley.
4. Mix it thoroughly before serving.

# Shrimp
# Tempura

Prep Time: 45 mins
Total Time: 1 hr

Servings per Recipe: 8
Calories              574 kcal
Carbohydrates         15.7 g
Cholesterol           124 mg
Fat                   48.3 g
Protein               11.4 g
Sodium                424 mg

## Ingredients

1/2 cup rice wine
1/4 tsp salt
1/2 pound fresh shrimp, peeled and deveined
2 quarts oil for deep frying
1/4 cup all-purpose flour
1/3 cup ice water
1/4 cup cornstarch

1 egg yolk
1/4 tsp salt
1/4 tsp white sugar
1 tsp shortening
1/2 tsp baking powder

## Directions

1. Coat shrimp with the mixture of rice wine and salt before refrigerating for at least 20 minutes.
2. Combine all-purpose flour, white sugar, ice water, cornstarch, egg yolk, salt, shortening and baking powder in a medium sized bowl.
3. Coat shrimp with this flour mixture before deep frying it in the hot oil for about 2 minutes or until you see that it is golden brown from all sides.
4. Drain with the help of paper towel.
5. Serve.

# EASY
# Italian Parmigiana

Prep Time: 30 mins
Total Time: 1 hr 30 mins

Servings per Recipe: 2
Calories          528 kcal
Fat               18.3 g
Carbohydrates     44.9 g
Protein           43.5 g
Cholesterol       184 mg
Sodium            1309 mg

## Ingredients

1 egg, beaten
2 oz. dry bread crumbs
2 skinless, boneless chicken breast halves
3/4 (16 oz.) jar spaghetti sauce

2 oz. shredded mozzarella cheese
1/4 C. grated Parmesan cheese

## Directions

1. Coat a cookie sheet with oil then set your oven to 350 degrees before doing anything else.
2. Get a bowl and add in your eggs.
3. Get a 2nd bowl and add in your bread crumbs.
4. Coat your chicken first with the eggs then with the bread crumbs.
5. Lay your pieces of chicken on the cookie sheet and cook them in the oven for 45 mins, until they are fully done.
6. Now add half of your pasta sauce to a casserole dish and lay in your chicken on top of the sauce.
7. Place the rest of the sauce on top of the chicken pieces. Then add a topping of parmesan and mozzarella over everything.
8. Cook the parmigiana in the oven for 25 mins.
9. Enjoy.

# Classical
# Sausage and Peppers from Italy

Prep Time: 15 mins
Total Time: 40 mins

Servings per Recipe: 6
Calories          461 kcal
Fat               39.4 g
Carbohydrates     7g
Protein           17.1 g
Cholesterol       96 mg
Sodium            857 mg

## Ingredients

6 (4 oz.) links sweet Italian sausage
2 tbsps butter
1 yellow onion, sliced
1/2 red onion, sliced
4 cloves garlic, minced
1 large red bell pepper, sliced
1 green bell pepper, sliced

1 tsp dried basil
1 tsp dried oregano
1/4 C. white wine

## Directions

1. Stir fry your sausage until it is fully browned then place the meat to side and cut it into pieces.
2. Now begin to stir fry the following for 5 mins, in butter, in the same pan: garlic, red onions, and yellow onions.
3. Now add in the bell peppers, white wine, oregano, and basil.
4. Let the mix continue to cook until the onions are soft.
5. Add the sausage back to the mix, set the heat to low, place a lid on the pan, and let the contents cook for 20 mins.
6. Enjoy.

# EASY
# Biscotti

Prep Time: 25 mins
Total Time: 1 hr 35 mins

Servings per Recipe: 30

| | |
|---|---|
| Calories | 138 kcal |
| Fat | 7.8 g |
| Carbohydrates | 15.5g |
| Protein | 2.2 g |
| Cholesterol | 25 mg |
| Sodium | 89 mg |

## Ingredients

3/4 C. butter
1 C. white sugar
2 eggs
1 1/2 tsps vanilla extract
2 1/2 C. all-purpose flour

1 tsp ground cinnamon
3/4 tsp baking powder
1/2 tsp salt
1 C. hazelnuts

## Directions

1.  Coat a baking dish with oil then set your oven to 350 degrees before doing anything else.
2.  Get a bowl, combine: sugar and butter. Mix the contents until it is creamy.
3.  Now add in the vanilla and the eggs. Stir the mix then sift in: salt, flour, baking powder, and cinnamon. Stir everything again then add in the hazelnuts.
4.  Now form your dough into 2 foot long cylinders.
5.  Lay the cylinders on the cookie sheet and flatten them.
6.  Let the dough cook in the oven for 35 mins. Then let the loaves lose their heat.
7.  Now cut each one diagonally and place everything back in the oven for 12 more mins.
8.  Flip the loaves after 6 mins of cooking.
9.  Enjoy.

# Italian
# Tuscan Soup

Prep Time: 15 mins
Total Time: 1 hr 10 mins

Servings per Recipe: 6
| | |
|---|---|
| Calories | 459 kcal |
| Fat | 34.1 g |
| Carbohydrates | 21.1g |
| Protein | 17.2 g |
| Cholesterol | 87 mg |
| Sodium | 1925 mg |

## Ingredients

1 (16 oz.) package smoked sausage
2 potatoes, cut into 1/4-inch slices
3/4 C. diced onion
6 slices bacon
1 1/2 tsps minced garlic
2 C. kale - washed, dried, and shredded
2 tbsps chicken bouillon powder

1 quart water
1/3 C. heavy whipping cream

## Directions

1. Set your oven to 300 degrees before doing anything else.
2. Place your pieces of sausage on a cookie sheet and cook everything in the oven for 30 mins.
3. Then divide the meat in half and then cut them in half again diagonally.
4. Begin to stir fry your bacon and onions until the onions are translucent then remove the bacon from the pan.
5. Add in the garlic and cook everything for 2 more mins then add the chicken base, potatoes, and water.
6. Let the mix gently boil for 20 mins then add in: the cream, bacon, kale, and sausage.
7. Let the soup cook for 5 mins.
8. Enjoy.

# BRUSCHETTA

Prep Time: 15 mins
Total Time: 35 mins

Servings per Recipe: 12

| | |
|---|---|
| Calories | 215 kcal |
| Fat | 8.9 g |
| Carbohydrates | 24.8g |
| Protein | 9.6 g |
| Cholesterol | 12 mg |
| Sodium | 426 mg |

## Ingredients

6 roma (plum) tomatoes, diced
1/2 C. sun-dried tomatoes, packed in oil
3 cloves minced garlic
1/4 C. olive oil
2 tbsps balsamic vinegar
1/4 C. fresh basil, stems removed

1/4 tsp salt
1/4 tsp ground black pepper
1 French baguette
2 C. shredded mozzarella cheese

## Directions

1. Get your oven's broiler hot before doing anything else.
2. Now grab a bowl, mix: pepper, roma tomatoes, salt, sun-dried tomatoes, basil, garlic, vinegar, and olive oil.
3. Let this mix sit for 12 mins and begin to slice your bread into 3/4 of inch pieces.
4. Place the pieces of bread on a cookie sheet then place everything under the broiler for 3 mins.
5. Now evenly top each piece of bread with the roma tomato mix.
6. Then add a piece of cheese on top of each one.
7. Cook the bread slices under the broiler for 6 more mins.
8. Enjoy.

# *Authentic*
# Eggplant Parmes

🥣 Prep Time: 25 mins
🕐 Total Time: 1 hr

Servings per Recipe: 10
Calories            487 kcal
Fat                 16 g
Carbohydrates       62.1g
Protein             24.2 g
Cholesterol         73 mg
Sodium              1663 mg

## Ingredients

3 eggplant, peeled and thinly sliced
2 eggs, beaten
4 C. Italian seasoned bread crumbs
6 C. spaghetti sauce, divided
1 (16 oz.) package mozzarella cheese, shredded and
divided

1/2 C. grated Parmesan cheese, divided
1/2 tsp dried basil

## Directions

1. Set your oven to 350 degrees before doing anything else.
2. Coat your pieces of eggplant with egg then with bread crumbs.
3. Now lay the veggies on a cookie sheet and cook them in the oven for 6 mins. Flip the eggplants and cook them for 6 more mins.
4. Coat the bottom of a casserole dish with pasta sauce then layer some of your eggplants in the dish.
5. Top the veggies with some parmesan and mozzarella then layer your eggplants, sauce, and cheese.
6. Continue this pattern until all the ingredients have been used up.
7. Finally coat the layer with some basil and cook everything in the oven for 40 mins. Enjoy.

# CLASSICAL
# Risotto

Prep Time: 20 mins
Total Time: 50 mins

Servings per Recipe: 6
| | |
|---|---|
| Calories | 431 kcal |
| Fat | 16.6 g |
| Carbohydrates | 56.6g |
| Protein | 11.3 g |
| Cholesterol | 29 mg |
| Sodium | 1131 mg |

## Ingredients

6 C. chicken broth, divided
3 tbsps olive oil, divided
1 lb portobello mushrooms, thinly sliced
1 lb white mushrooms, thinly sliced
2 shallots, diced
1 1/2 C. Arborio rice
1/2 C. dry white wine

sea salt to taste
freshly ground black pepper to taste
3 tbsps finely diced chives
4 tbsps butter
1/3 C. freshly grated Parmesan cheese

## Directions

1.  Get your broth warm with a low level of heat. Then begin to stir fry your mushrooms in 2 tbsp of olive oil for 4 mins.
2.  Now remove everything from the pot and add in 1 more tbsp of olive oil and begin to fry your shallots in it for 2 mins then add in the rice and stir fry it for 3 mins.
3.  Pour in the wine while continuing to stir, and keep stirring, until it is absorbed.
4.  Once the wine has been absorbed combine in half a C. of broth and keep stirring until it is absorbed as well.
5.  Now for about 20 mins keep pouring in half a C. of broth and stirring the mix until the broth is absorbed by the rice.
6.  After 20 mins of forming the risotto, shut the heat and combine in: the parmesan, pepper, mushrooms and their juice, chives, salt, and butter.
7.  Enjoy.

# *Tortellini*
# Classico

🥣 Prep Time: 20 mins

🕐 Total Time: 1 hr 35 mins

Servings per Recipe: 8

| | |
|---|---|
| Calories | 324 kcal |
| Fat | 20.2 g |
| Carbohydrates | 19.1g |
| Protein | 14.6 g |
| Cholesterol | 50 mg |
| Sodium | 1145 mg |

## Ingredients

1 lb sweet Italian sausage, casings removed
1 C. diced onion
2 cloves garlic, minced
5 C. beef broth
1/2 C. water
1/2 C. red wine
4 large tomatoes - peeled, seeded and diced
1 C. thinly sliced carrots

1/2 tbsp packed fresh basil leaves
1/2 tsp dried oregano
1 (8 oz.) can tomato sauce
1 1/2 C. sliced zucchini
8 oz. fresh tortellini pasta
3 tbsps diced fresh parsley

## Directions

1. In a large pot brown your sausage all over.
2. Then remove the meat from the pan.
3. Begin to stir fry your garlic and onions in the drippings then add in: the sausage, broth, tomato sauce, water, oregano, wine, basil, tomatoes, and carrots.
4. Get the mix boiling, set the heat to low, and let everything cook for 35 mins.
5. Remove any fat which rises to the top then add in the parsley and zucchini.
6. Continue cooking the mix for 20 more mins before adding in the pasta and letting everything cooking 15 more mins.
7. When serving the dish top it with parmesan.
8. Enjoy.

# FETA
# Fettucine

Prep Time: 15 mins
Total Time: 25 mins

Servings per Recipe: 4
| | |
|---|---|
| Calories | 663 kcal |
| Fat | 39.4 g |
| Carbohydrates | 64.8g |
| Protein | 16.5 g |
| Cholesterol | 11 mg |
| Sodium | 248 mg |

## Ingredients

1 bunch diced fresh cilantro
6 tbsps pine nuts
1 tsp lemon juice, or to taste
1/3 C. crumbled feta cheese
salt and ground black pepper to taste

1/2 C. olive oil
1 (12 oz.) package fettucine pasta
1 tsp extra-virgin olive oil

## Directions

1. Pulse the following in a food processor until minced: black pepper, cilantro, salt, pine nuts, feta cheese, and lemon juice.
2. Now slowly add in half a C. of olive oil while continually running the processor.
3. Boil your pasta for 9 mins in water and salt then remove the liquids.
4. Place the pasta in a bowl and top it with the cilantro sauce.
5. Toss the mix then add some olive oil and toss everything again.
6. Enjoy.

# *Authentic*
# Meatball Sub

🥄 Prep Time: 15 mins
🕐 Total Time: 1 hr 40 mins

Servings per Recipe: 6
| | |
|---|---|
| Calories | 491 kcal |
| Fat | 21.4 g |
| Carbohydrates | 43.1g |
| Protein | 29.3 g |
| Cholesterol | 75 mg |
| Sodium | 1068 mg |

## Ingredients

1 1/2 lbs lean ground beef
1/3 C. Italian seasoned bread crumbs
1/2 small onion, diced
1 tsp salt
1/2 C. shredded mozzarella cheese, divided
1 tbsp cracked black pepper

1 tsp garlic powder
1/2 C. marinara sauce
3 hoagie rolls, split lengthwise

## Directions

1. Set your oven to 350 degrees before doing anything else.
2. Get a bowl, combine: 1/2 of the mozzarella, beef, garlic powder, bread crumbs, pepper, onions, and salt.
3. Shape the mix into a large loaf then place it in a casserole dish.
4. Cook the meat in the oven for 55 mins then let it cool for 10 mins.
5. Cut the meat into slices then layer the pieces of meat on a roll.
6. Top everything with the marinara then add a topping of cheese.
7. Cover the sandwich with some foil and put everything in the oven for 20 more mins.
8. Let the sandwich cool for 20 mins then cut each one in half.
9. Enjoy.

# AUTHENTIC
# Calamari

🥘 Prep Time: 20 mins
🕐 Total Time: 40 mins

Servings per Recipe: 6
| | |
|---|---|
| Calories | 1019 kcal |
| Fat | 65.6 g |
| Carbohydrates | 141.7g |
| Protein | 65.6 g |
| Cholesterol | 1479 mg |
| Sodium | 11549 mg |

## Ingredients

12 calamari tubes, cleaned and dried
2 green onions, finely diced
6 cloves garlic, minced
1/2 lb diced cooked shrimp meat
1/2 lb cooked crabmeat, diced
1 tbsp lemon juice
3/4 C. butter
12 oz. cream cheese, cut into cubes

2 cloves garlic, minced
3 C. milk
10 oz. freshly grated Parmesan cheese
1 pinch ground black pepper
3/4 C. freshly grated Romano cheese
1 (8 oz.) package linguine pasta

## Directions

1. Set your oven to 350 degrees before doing anything else.
2. Get a bowl, combine: lemon juice, onions, crabmeat, 6 pieces of garlic, and shrimp.
3. Divide this mix amongst your tubes of squid then stake the tubes closed with a toothpick.
4. Place everything into a casserole dish.
5. Begin to heat and stir 2 cloves of garlic and cream cheese in butter until the cheese is melted.
6. Slowly add in your milk and keep stirring until all the milk is hot and everything is smooth.
7. Now add the pepper and parmesan.
8. Top the contents of the casserole dish with this mix. Then add 2 tbsp of Romano over everything.
9. Cook the mix in the oven until the cheese has melted and is browned.
10. At the same time begin to boil your pasta in water and salt for 9 mins then remove the liquid.
11. Serve the calamad over the pasta with a liber amount of sauce. Enjoy.

# Northern California
# Cioppino (Mussel and Clam Italian Stew)

Prep Time: 10 mins
Total Time: 55 mins

Servings per Recipe: 13
Calories          318 kcal
Fat               12.9 g
Carbohydrates     9.3g
Protein           34.9 g
Cholesterol       164 mg
Sodium            755 mg

## Ingredients

3/4 C. butter
2 onions, diced
2 cloves garlic, minced
1 bunch fresh parsley, diced
2 (14.5 oz.) cans stewed tomatoes
2 (14.5 oz.) cans chicken broth
2 bay leaves
1 tbsp dried basil
1/2 tsp dried thyme
1/2 tsp dried oregano
1 C. water

1 1/2 C. white wine
1 1/2 lbs large shrimp - peeled and deveined
1 1/2 lbs bay scallops
18 small clams
18 mussels, cleaned and debearded
1 1/2 C. crabmeat
1 1/2 lbs cod fillets, cubed

## Directions

1.  Stir fry your parsley, garlic, and onions, in butter, in a large pot.
2.  Cook the mix until the onions are tender.
3.  Now combine in the tomatoes, wine, broth, water, bay leaves, thyme, basil, and oregano.
4.  Place a lid on the pot and let the mix gently boil for 35 mins.
5.  Now add in the crab, shrimp, mussels, clams, and scallops.
6.  Stir the mix then add in the fish.
7.  Get everything boiling then place the lid back on the pot and let the contents cook for 9 more mins until the clams open.
8.  Divide the mix between bowls then top each with bread. Enjoy.

# CLASSICAL
# Fettuccine

Prep Time: 15 mins

Total Time: 30 mins

Servings per Recipe: 4

| | |
|---|---|
| Calories | 651 kcal |
| Fat | 28.5 g |
| Carbohydrates | 52.2g |
| Protein | 43.8 g |
| Cholesterol | 266 mg |
| Sodium | 357 mg |

## Ingredients

8 oz. dry fettuccine pasta
3 cloves garlic
1/2 sweet onion, cut into wedges
3 tbsps fresh oregano leaves
4 tbsps olive oil
4 medium tomatoes, diced
3 tbsps diced fresh basil
salt and pepper to taste

1 C. spinach leaves
1 lb cooked shrimp - peeled and deveined
8 oz. fresh mozzarella cheese, diced

## Directions

1. Cook your pasta in water and salt for 9 mins then remove all the liquids.
2. Pulse the following a few times with a food processor: oregano, onion, and garlic.
3. Once the mix is minced begin to stir fry it in olive oil until everything is browned then add in: the pepper, tomatoes, salt, and basil.
4. Let the mix cook for 7 mins.
5. Now add in the spinach to the mix and let everything wilt then combine in the shrimp.
6. Get everything hot then add in the pasta and the mozzarella and stir the mix.
7. Enjoy.

# *Plum*
# Tomato and Olive Filets

🥣 Prep Time: 15 mins
🕐 Total Time: 45 mins

Servings per Recipe: 4
| | |
|---|---|
| Calories | 282 kcal |
| Fat | 15.4 g |
| Carbohydrates | 8.2g |
| Protein | 24.4 g |
| Cholesterol | 63 mg |
| Sodium | 777 mg |

## Ingredients

5 roma (plum) tomatoes
2 tbsps extra virgin olive oil
1/2 Spanish onion, diced
2 cloves garlic, diced
1 pinch Italian seasoning
24 kalamata olives, pitted and diced
1/4 C. white wine
1/4 C. capers

1 tsp fresh lemon juice
6 leaves fresh basil, diced
3 tbsps freshly grated Parmesan cheese
1 lb flounder fillets
6 leaves fresh basil, torn

## Directions

1. Get a large pot of water boiling.
2. Once the water is boiling add in your tomatoes and let the tomatoes sit in the water for 10 secs then remove them to a bowl of water and ice.
3. Once the tomatoes have cooled remove the skins and dice them.
4. Now begin to stir fry your onions in olive oil for 7 mins then add in the Italian seasoning, tomatoes, and garlic.
5. Let the mix cook for 9 mins then combine in: 1/2 of the basil, olives, lemon juice, wine, and capers.
6. Set the heat to low then mix in the parmesan.
7. Let the contents cook for 17 mins with a low heat.
8. Now place your fish in a casserole dish, pour in the sauce, add the rest of the basil, and put everything in the oven for 14 mins. Enjoy.

# CHICKEN
# Cutlets

🥘 Prep Time: 10 mins

🕐 Total Time: 20 mins

Servings per Recipe: 4

| | |
|---|---|
| Calories | 297 kcal |
| Carbohydrates | 22.2 g |
| Cholesterol | 118 mg |
| Fat | 11.4 g |
| Protein | 31.2 g |
| Sodium | 251 mg |

## Ingredients

4 skinless, boneless chicken breast halves - pounded
to 1/2 inch thickness
2 tbsps all-purpose flour
1 egg, beaten

1 cup panko bread crumbs
1 cup oil for frying, or as needed

## Directions

1. Get three bowls. Bowl 1 for chicken. Bowl 2 for bread crumbs. Bowl 3 for eggs.
2. Cover chicken with flour first. Then with egg, and finally with crumbs.
3. Get a frying pan and heat 1/4 inch of oil. Fry your chicken for 5 mins on each side.
4. Remove excess oil.
5. Enjoy

Printed in Great Britain
by Amazon

23696828R00031